IMAGES
of America

URSULINE SISTERS
OF GREAT FALLS

IMAGES
of America

URSULINE SISTERS
OF GREAT FALLS

Sister Francis Xavier Porter, O.S.U.
and Kristi D. Scott

ARCADIA
PUBLISHING

Published by Arcadia Publishing
Charleston, South Carolina

Library of Congress Control Number: 2012934472

For all general information, please contact Arcadia Publishing:
Telephone 843-853-2070
Fax 843-853-0044
E-mail sales@arcadiapublishing.com
For customer service and orders:
Toll-Free 1-888-313-2665

Visit us on the Internet at www.arcadiapublishing.com

To St. Angela Merici, in honor of her devotion, dedication, great love for God, and service to God's people, and to all those who have become captivated and motivated by her efforts

CONTENTS

FOREWORD

Over 100 years have passed since the Order of Ursuline Sisters (OSU) constructed their grand building on a slight hill in the city of Great Falls, Montana. Their building has served as an academy of education and a boarding school for hundreds of students. It also functioned as a motherhouse for all of the Ursuline Missions in Montana. The OSU archives became repositories for work and activities over the past century and include accounts from Idaho, Alaska, and Montana. This initial photographic research project seeks to reconnect the public with visual forms of memory that contribute to our understanding of Montana Ursulines' history, particularly in Great Falls. These records are still intact and stand as testimony to the sisters' role in education across the continent. With more time and attention to these stories, they no doubt will take on renewed significance. In addition, further examination of Ursuline archival-based research is warranted, as is a more complete history of Ursuline Centre. The intersecting lives of Ursuline superiors, sisters, students, instructors, associates, staff members, and friends are truly boundless. The authors are grateful to Ursuline archivists, historians, and the supportive public that remains interested in the ministry and cultural legacy granted through the efforts of Ursuline sisters. Their vision and devotion to the preservation of their own heritage and our shared regional history is commendable. We would like to thank our editor at Arcadia Publishing, Elizabeth Bray, for her numerous consultations, pep talks, and patience. We also thank local historian Ken Robison for his consultation on the project. Ursuline Centre in Great Falls has been truly blessed with wonderful and supportive family and friends who have spent countless hours volunteering, laboring, supporting, and inspiring those involved. I personally thank Sr. Francis Xavier Porter for her dedication to the love of God and people that has fueled her own ministry and especially for her patience in my novice attempts to comprehend both the Ursulines' local and worldwide history of nearly 500 years. Her willingness to examine this partial history with me and share it with the community is much appreciated. Also, her progressive nature with technology has spurred the inaugural digitization project with Ursuline archives, further preserving the images contained in this book and making them more assessable. Unless otherwise noted, all images appear courtesy of the Ursuline Western Province Archives in Great Falls, Montana.

—Kristi D. Scott

INTRODUCTION

In 16th-century Italy, Angela Merici gathered a group of young women who shared her love for God and her desire to serve. They lived in their own homes, and from there, they did various charitable works and regularly gathered together to pray and to learn. The structure she gave them included both spiritual and practical norms. From this beginning, other groups were formed, some with the same unstructured style and some with the formal structure of a monastery. The monastic form became that of the Ursuline communities in much of Europe. Angela had advised her followers, "And if, according to times and circumstances, the need arises to make new rules or do something differently, do it prudently and with good advice." This account attempts to show ways Ursuline sisters have followed her advice in Great Falls, Montana. In 1639, a monastery in Tours, France, sent sisters to Quebec to share the gospel and to serve the needs of people in America—the Native Americans and the European settlers. The leader of these first Ursulines to come to the New World was Mother Marie of the Incarnation Guyart, a holy woman whose name is still well known in Eastern Canada. Later, other monasteries in Europe sent sisters to establish schools in America.

In 1884, six sisters from a convent in Toledo, Ohio, answered an appeal from the bishop in Montana to live and work among the native people in that territory. Mother Amadeus Dunne was the leader of this group. Their work in Montana began in Miles City and then spread to the Northern Cheyenne people on the Tongue River. Requests for help multiplied, the number of sisters increased, and within a few years, eight missions were established throughout Montana. St. Peter's, near present-day Cascade, became the motherhouse of several Montana foundations. Here, the sisters joined the Jesuit priests in operating schools for native and nonnative boys and girls. In 1908, when a fire destroyed several of the structures at St. Peter's, the sisters prayed and contemplated the request of Bishop Mathias C. Lenihan to open a boarding school in Great Falls. Permission was obtained from Ursuline superiors in Rome to move the motherhouse from St. Peter's to Great Falls. For a time, the Native American girls remained at St. Peter's, but after a second fire in 1918, they transferred to other mission schools. In Great Falls, Bishop Lenihan announced that a $100,000 girls' school would be erected.

John G. Morony offered the nuns city lots, and two were selected on Central Avenue. George Shanley was chosen as architect, and Leighland Kleppe and Company of Glasgow became contractor. The bid was $99,650, not including plumbing, wiring, or heating. The cornerstone of Ursuline Academy was laid on September 17, 1911, during a ceremony presided over by the bishop. Additional property was donated by the Great Falls Townsite Company. The school then occupied a $200,000 plant, totaling four city blocks. Doors opened to the first class in September 1912 for girls and boys, kindergarten through 12th grade. The building housed the Ursuline Sisters' motherhouse, and girls of school age were accepted as boarders.

For some years, the school had a few hundred day students and fifty or more boarding students. In 1925, the need for expansion necessitated a separate gymnasium and then an extension to the new gymnasium to provide living space for small boys. State accreditation was received in 1913. Along with a complete academic and commercial curriculum, education in the arts was highly emphasized. In 1934, the school became a member of both the North Central and the Northwestern Associations of Secondary Schools.

In addition to operating an academy, the sisters provided retreats for students and members of the ladies auxiliary. During the summer, they hosted an annual retreat for the priests of the diocese and taught religious education classes in several of the rural parishes. They also attended college and university classes to further their teaching skills.

As local Great Falls parishes established parochial schools, and the diocese built a central high school, the sisters exchanged their teaching at the academy for travel to teach in these other institutions. By the mid-1940s, calls to meet new needs again challenged the Ursuline Sisters. Only the kindergarten remained in the academy building. After much prayerful discernment and research, during a time of hardship, faithful friends helped sisters recognize an unmet need. In 1971, the retreat ministry expanded. The academy building, long an integral part of the Great Falls area, gradually became the place for conferences, meetings, and other types of local activities, which enabled the Ursuline Sisters, dedicated staff, and volunteers to reach out to the community.

The academy building, a historical treasure, is listed on the National Register of Historic Places. The academy's museum houses historical, ethnographic materials particular to the cultures of Montana dating from the Ursuline Sisters' time on the Indian missions approximately between 1900 and 1950. Also displayed is much from the days of the academy and college. Over the years, the literary collection and archival materials have accumulated. Ursuline Academy/Centre continues to contribute a place for early childhood education, for sacred space to pray and share, and for religious and community meetings.

The design of the building speaks to the vision of both the architect and the founding Ursuline sisters. In the beginning, in 1912, it served well as a state-of-the-art boarding school and later continued to serve as a school for students of various ages, then as a facility for meetings, retreats, overnight conferences, and other public service groups. Throughout its history, the chapel has remained the heart of both the ministry of the Ursuline Sisters and of the building itself.

Ursuline sisters throughout the world have a rich history of working with and empowering others to carry on their apostolic ministries. This is part of their tradition, and in keeping with it, the various ministries here in Montana have been given over to the hands of others. In 1995, the operation of Ursuline Centre was transferred from the sisters to a board of trustees, which employs a lay director. Looking to the future, the value of keeping the ministry alive is apparent. It is the only retreat and conference center in the area, and the building contributes significant historical and cultural value to the region. To provide for this, the Ursuline Sisters are now in the process of transferring ownership to the Ursuline Centre Historical Foundation, founded in 1996. Ursuline Centre Historical Foundation has invested over $2 million in the maintenance and restoration of this wonderful historical building that has graced the city of Great Falls for a century.

Encouraging spiritual and educational growth, the center strives to meet the current and future needs of the people of the Great Falls region just as the Ursuline Sisters have for generations past.

Pictures and captions in this book highlight some events and a few persons from the beginning of Ursuline to its present state in Great Falls, Montana. It is not a complete history.

One

BEGINNINGS

St. Angela Merici looked beyond the traditional choices for women in 16th-century Europe. Completely dedicated to love for God and serving others, she gathered a group of young women who aspired to the same. They lived in their homes and came together regularly for prayer and instruction. Unique among founders, St. Angela directed her followers to make changes when needed. (Calligraphy courtesy of Sr. Theresa Eppridge, OSU.)

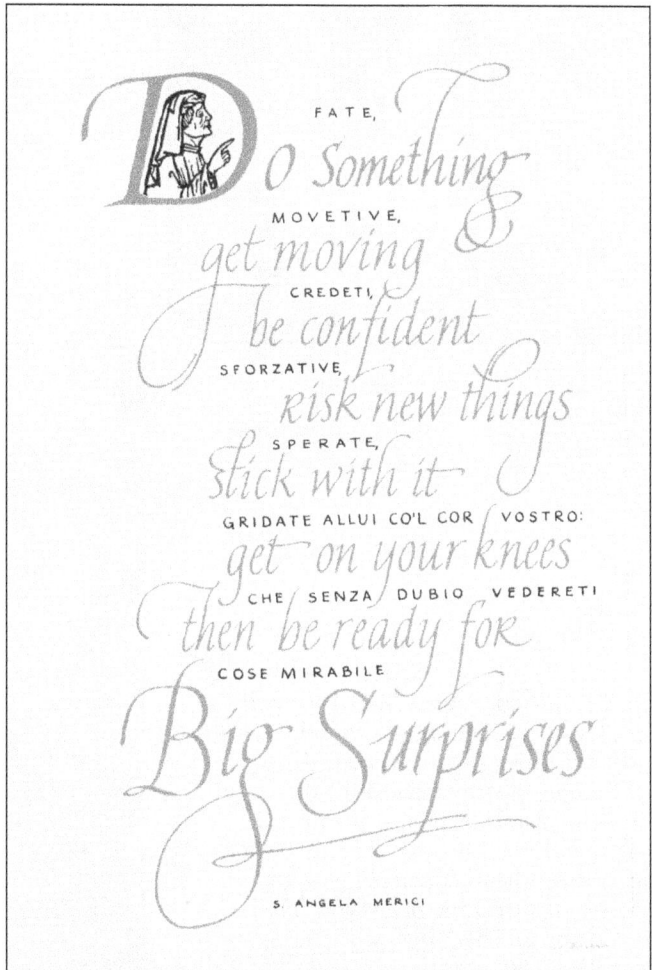

FATE,
Do something
MOVETIVE,
get moving
CREDETI,
be confident
SFORZATIVE,
risk new things
SPERATE,
stick with it
GRIDATE ALLUI CO'L COR VOSTRO:
get on your knees
CHE SENZA DUBIO VEDERETI
then be ready for
COSE MIRABILE
Big Surprises

S. ANGELA MERICI

St. Ursula, a courageous woman of fifth-century Britton, gave her life for love of God. She and virgin companions on a pilgrimage to holy places across Europe were martyred rather than give up their virginity. Since she lived in the fifth century, much of her life story is legend. It was her spirit as a valiant woman that inspired St. Angela when she learned about her in the 16th century.

As a young girl, Angela Merici was part of a loving family in northern Italy on the southern shores of Lake Garda. While still young, she experienced the death of several family members. She prayed particularly for some sign that her beloved sister was in heaven, and her prayer was answered in the form of a vision. The vision also told her God's wish that she would found a company of women.

A few decades later in 1535 in Brescia, Italy, after years of prayer, fasting, and serving the townspeople in various ways, St. Angela gathered together a group of women. They were to live a consecrated life in their own homes, to adapt no specific mission, but serve people as needed. Needs were plentiful in 16th-century Brescia during the time of the Reformation.

Throughout her life, St. Angela spent long hours in prayer and fasting. She prepared a simple, clearly defined set of rules and counsels for her company. There were three sections to her writings. The rules applied to everyone. Counsels were directed to those who would be the leaders. In a collection of legacies, St. Angela provided directives and insurances of God's guidance to those in charge of governing.

After her death, St. Angela's company grew and spread rapidly throughout Italy and later in France, where the communities took on a monastic form, including cloister. St. Charles Borromeo, archbishop of Milan, played a large part in the expansion and reorganization. A few examples of these large monasteries were Calvi in Umbria, Italy, and Tours and Paris in France. In the Ursuline monasteries, education of young women became the principle ministry. At the same time, communities of sisters living according to the same lifestyle as St. Angela increased in number, primarily in Italy.

Institution Sainte-Ursule.   SAINT-POL-DE-LÉON. — La Chapelle.

Ursuline Boarding School, Tournai, Belgium.

Façade et cour d'entrée.

Expansion of Ursuline monasteries across the globe continued and soon included Belgium, Holland, Germany, and lands beyond Europe. Missionaries from the European monasteries went to such places as Java (Indonesia) and Siam (Thailand). The goal, as it had been for St. Angela, was to share the Gospel message and serve the needs of the people. At the same time, the simple, unstructured lifestyle begun by St. Angela in Brescia, Italy, continued to flourish in some places.

"CARITAS CHRISTI URGET NOS"

S. ANGELA MERICIA VOB...

TRANSVAAL ALASKA, JAVA, SIAM, CHINA EN BRAZILIE.

Lou Asperslagh fec.

QUAERITE PRIMUM REGNUM DEI.

« Kunst-Adelt » Maastricht.   Nadruk verboden.

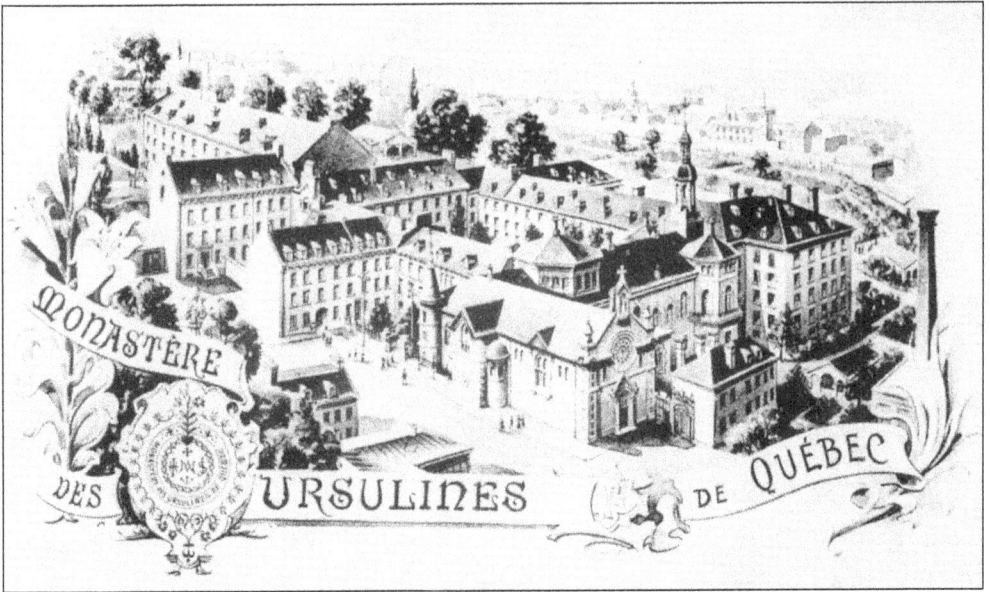

In 1639, from the monastery in Tours, France, Mother Marie of the Incarnation Guyart and companions came to Quebec, Canada. Their purpose was to share the gospel message with people in the New World, both the indigenous people and the European settlers or immigrants. Mother Marie of the Incarnation Guyart was a very holy woman who continually prayed to be able to bring the whole world to God. She was gifted with a vision of the work God wished her to do in the New World.

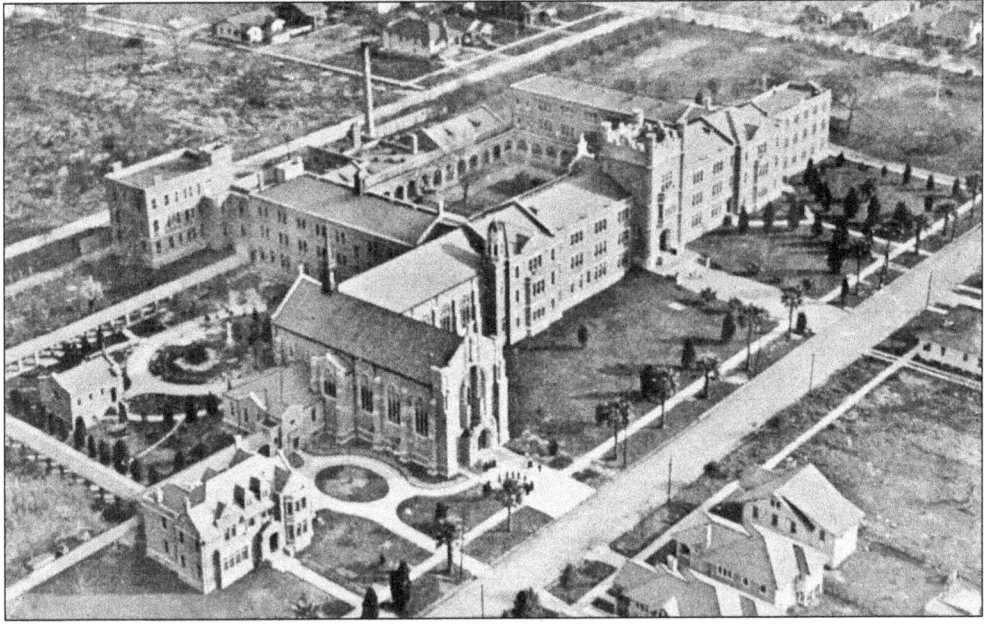

Ursuline sisters came to the French colony of New Orleans in 1727. They established the first Catholic school in what became the United States. Ursuline history in this area includes the first classes for female slaves, free women, and Native Americans. Their school also provided opportunities for spiritual and cultural development of the young ladies of the aristocracy. An Ursuline academy continues to operate in New Orleans.

Washington May 15 1804.

To the Soeur Therese de S.t xavier farjon Superior, and the Nuns of the order of S.t Ursula at new Orleans.

I have recieved, holy sisters, the letter you have written me wherein you express anxiety for the property vested in your institution by the former governments of Louisiana. the principles of the constitution. and government of the United states are a sure guarantee to you that it will be preserved to you sacred and inviolate, and that your institution will be permitted to govern itself according to it's own voluntary rules, without interference from the civil authority. whatever diversity of shade may appear in the religious opinions of our fellow citizens, the charitable objects of your institution cannot be indifferent to any; and it's further-ance of the wholesome purposes of society, by training up it's younger members in the way they should go, cannot fail to ensure it the patronage of the government it is under. be assured it will meet all the protection which my office can give it.

I salute you, holy sisters, with friendship & respect.

Th: Jefferson

From the time of their arrival in New Orleans, the Ursuline Sisters recognized and served the needs of the city. When the ownership of the territory changed from France to the United States, the sisters were given a letter of guarantee from President Jefferson as to the ownership of their property and school in New Orleans. The people of the city appreciated the care and generosity of the sisters as they lived out the ideals of St. Ursula and their founder, St. Angela. (Courtesy of Ursuline Archives, New Orleans.)

RT. REV. BISHOP GILMOUR.

Ursuline sisters responded to requests from bishops in other parts of the United States. The convent in Toledo, Ohio, had its beginning in the diocese of Cleveland, Ohio. It was from this place that Ursuline sisters came to Montana. As a result of the Indian Wars, the Northern Cheyenne people had lost some of the most fruitful of their land. Some caring people in the military and the Catholic Church looked for some solution. Bishop Jean-Baptiste Brondel of Montana petitioned Bishop Richard Gilmour of Cleveland, Ohio, for some sisters to work among the Northern Cheyenne. It was thought that religious women would help to calm the rapidly declining situation in the unorganized territories that would become the state of Montana. Six Ursulines of the convent in Toledo were accepted as volunteers to begin this work.

On January 18, 1884, Ursuline missionaries arrived in Miles City, Montana, via the new railroad. Pictured here is the young leader, Mother Amadeus Dunne. Born in Akron, Ohio, in 1844, she professed vows as an Ursuline in 1864. She had previously served as superior in the Ursuline convent in Ohio and was well recognized as a natural leader.

Pictured are the six Ursuline sisters who left Toledo for Montana in 1884. They are, from left to right (first row) Ignatius McFarland, Amadeus Dunne, and Sacred Heart Meilink; (second row) Angela Abair, Francis Seibert, and Holy Angels Carabin. Their destination was the encampment of the Northern Cheyenne along the Tongue River, but they were able to travel by train only as far as Miles City, Montana. (Courtesy of Ursuline Archives, Toledo, Ohio.)

Upon arrival in Miles City, the first task of the six Ursulines was to search for suitable lodging. They found a small home with five rooms on the edge of town and started immediately to give lessons in order to support themselves. For some years, Miles City provided some support for the sisters working on the missions.

Over the years, some Ursuline sisters remained in Miles City, built a sizable convent, and conducted a boarding school. Sisters in this convent taught school, provided for boarding students, and gave a large number of music lessons. As far as they were able, the Miles City sisters helped fellow Ursuline sisters on the missions.

Old Catholic Mission, Tongue River, Montana

Above, this early postcard features Ursuline mission St. Labre on the Tongue River near Ashland. From the beginning, life at St. Labre was very hard, and the government provided little support for the Northern Cheyenne children. Years later, due to many generous benefactors, the mission expanded and now includes a school, boarding facilities, a chapel, and other buildings. In the photograph at right, Sr. Magdeline LaTrouche poses with four eighth-grade students. This mission was the only one founded and operated solely by the Ursulines for almost 50 years. They were replaced by Franciscan priests and sisters. It now has a lay director, Curtis Yarlott. (Above, photograph by Laton A. Huffman of Miles City, Montana.)

Pictured above is an Ursuline sister with an unidentified Native American family posing in front of a wagon. The woman on the left holds a horse by the reins, and a teepee can be seen in the background. This photograph was found in a box of Sr. Genevieve McBride's materials. McBride was an Ursuline sister and an avid historian.

In 1891, the Ursulines joined the Jesuits at St. Paul's Mission on the Fort Belknap Reservation in the Little Rockies. The campus encompassed many buildings, including the school, separate dormitories for boys and girls, and a church. Pictured here are a group of students with Mothers Cecilia Wiegard and Camilla Fouts. Some buildings, including the church, were destroyed by fire in 1931, yet the church and some of the other needed structures were rebuilt. The school continues to flourish today, staffed by Dominican sisters and Jesuit volunteers, still under the spiritual leadership of Jesuit priests.

Blackfeet tribal members process during the dedication of the new church at Holy Family Mission in the photograph above. Such an occasion was cause for the many families converted to Catholicism on the reservation to celebrate. A generous gift from Katherine Drexel made this mission possible. Katherine Drexel, a wealthy woman in Philadelphia, was dedicated to helping others. She had been most generous to several of the Ursuline missions and later founded a congregation of sisters to serve Native Americans and African Americans. The photograph below shows a group of young boys posing for a photograph near one of the buildings at Holy Family Mission.

The First General Chapter of Ursuline sisters met in Rome in 1900. Pope Leo XIII had invited representatives from the entire world to meet and consider joining together. Sharing personnel and finances would then be a greater possibility. An "x" identifies Mother Amadeus Dunne of the Montana Ursulines in the second row. Seated in the first row is Mary Kolenzuten, the young Blackfeet girl Mother Amadeus brought with her. She was also known as Marie Stewart, daughter of Granville Stewart, the territorial governor of Montana.

Two

ST. PETER'S MISSION

In 1884, the first buildings at St. Peter's Mission for the sisters and girls included the chapel and a bell tower. They lived in these cabins for some time until a stone building was erected. Seated in the wagon is Mary Fields, an African American woman who came from Toledo to Montana to help nurse Mother Amadeus back to health. She stayed on and helped the sisters in many ways.

The Jesuit boys' building is pictured here at St. Peter's Mission. The mission was situated near the Mullan Road, the primary route to Fort Benton on the Missouri River. The Jesuits moved the mission here from another location in 1865, and soldiers at nearby Fort Shaw guarded the road. Various buttes and other geographic features are shown in the background. The original structures at the mission are shown in the background, including the chapel and bell tower.

Over 40 boys dressed alike pose in front of a building that is surrounded by a picket fence. There is a man on a horse in the background and a priest in the middle of the group. A few men flank the group, and two people lean against a fence in the background. After the Jesuits left St. Peter's, the Ursulines took on the boys' schools as well.

This bird's-eye view of St. Peter's mission shows most of the campus, including the Ursuline buildings and the Jesuit buildings. A laundry, bake house, chicken yard, worker's barn, opera house, and corral are among other structures pictured nestled in the valley. Today, only rubble remains of the buildings.

The Ursuline sisters' grand stone building served as classrooms and dormitories for the sisters and for children. The school was known as the Mount Angela Ursuline Academy and was three stories in height. The motherhouse for the Ursuline Sisters of Montana was originally located here. Mother Amadeus Dunne resided here as well, and all gatherings of sisters from the other missions took place at this location.

Pictured above are five Ursuline novices seated amongst eight Ursuline sisters, including Mother Amadeus Dunne. Two aspirants and one small child with Mother Amadeus in the center are also in the group. St. Peter's included both Native American and white children as students. Boys and girls were separated, as were Native Americans from whites. At one time, the sisters had all four schools, each with differing curriculum and needs.

A group of nuns and students pose on a hillside near St. Peter's Mission with prominent geographic features identified in the background. Patches of snow spot the ground, and the women wear long wool coats. Although the sisters' original wish was to work with the Native American people, they accepted and educated white children of the settlers in the area.

An inscription on the back of this photograph taken at St. Peter's Mission reads, "One of the sisters recalls the faces of these girls but is not sure of their names. Among first graduate Native American girls of St. Peter's." Mother Francis Siebert is identified as the nun in the photograph that was likely taken before 1887.

Three Native American students pose alongside the Ursuline's stone building at St. Peter's. All three wear identical uniforms and similar-style shoes. Their hair is pulled back and styled. At this period in history, it was thought by many that helping the indigenous people included teaching them the manner of dress of white children. Acculturation of Native children was a priority to both missionary and government schools.

A group of young musicians pose for a photograph with their instruments at St. Peter's Mission. Pictured with them are Ursuline sisters Annunciata Dunne and Amata Dunne. These blood sisters were nieces of Mother Amadeus Dunne, the founder of the Montana missions. Music and learning to play a stringed instrument was an important and enjoyable part of the curriculum. Many of the students became quite proficient in music. The instruments were among the items the sisters asked their benefactors to send them.

Mother Agnus Dunne instructs a class of high school students at St. Peter's Mission. A potbelly stove warms the small classroom. Note that George Washington and the date, February 22, 1901, are written across the blackboard. This appears to be a typical Ursuline classroom at St. Peter's Mission.

The date is written across the blackboard in the background, February 14, 1901, and students work with various techniques and mediums of art projects. An Ursuline teacher sits in the back of this classroom at St. Peter's Mission; a label indicates that the photograph is of a pyrography class. The students from left to right are Mable Manny, Nora Moran, Jessie Clark, Ursula Mason, and Lorena Dawson.

The first graduates of St. Peter's in 1902 are, from left to right, Lorena Dawson, Pearl White, Margaret Moran, Winifred Cloeman, Mabel Mannix, Mary Hollenback, and Mabel O'Connell. They pose proudly with their diplomas in formal attire in a room decorated for the purpose. Each graduate's name is written faintly in pencil on the back of the photograph.

Physical activity was included in the curriculum. Seven Native American students pose in sneakers with one holding the basketball. The individuals are labeled with a number that corresponds to their names written on the back of the photograph. The basketball players from left to right are (first row) Marie Big Beaver; (second row) Thecla Medicine Bird, Mary Red Beads, Maratha Walks Along, Clara Wooden Thigh, Gladys Wolf Black, and Mary Swallow.

Pictured in 1900, the altar and tabernacle are elaborately decorated in the chapel of the sisters' convent at St. Peter's. There are several statues of angels. Stations of the Cross line the wall. Note the gas light fixtures in the ceiling. There are individual kneelers but no chairs or benches. Sections of carpet cover the aisle and parts of the floor.

A group of female students dressed for First Communion pose with the priest. Religious instruction was an important part of life at the mission, and it was the Ursuline Sisters' primary purpose for being there. First Communion was a significant step in spiritual development, so the event was honored with special celebration.

Girls from St. Peter's Academy, dressed in their Sunday best, pose on the front steps of the large stone building. As part of their education in Christianity, Sunday was a day for special prayers and recreational activities.

Students line up in front of the stone building at St Peter's. They are dressed alike in plaid uniforms. The Ursulines' boarding school for Native American children grew from around 12 students to nearly 200 at its height in the 1890s. Preparation for future life in the Euro-American world included dressing according to that culture and other forms of acculturation that are no longer acceptable.

Children and sisters practice stringed instruments in the music room at the mission. Large maps hang from the walls, and a piano and an organ can be seen. This is a classic image for the sisters in their various missions and schools. Music and art were emphasized, in addition to basic and advanced academia. Many of the sisters themselves were accomplished musicians and in turn taught their students.

Five students stand against the blackboard that is decorated with a banner and instructions for "photograph writing." This may have been a typical classroom at Mount Angela Ursuline Academy at St. Peter's Mission. The image was taken between 1884, when the Ursuline Sisters joined the Jesuits there, and 1912, when the remainder of the sisters' belongings were moved to Ursuline Academy in the nearby city of Great Falls.

A small child poses beside an ornately carved chair. The Ursuline Sisters brought a specialist from the East to teach them to carve, and the sisters in turn taught the children. A few samples of these fine carvings are in the Heritage Museum at Ursuline Centre.

Sr. Amata Dunne poses with students in an art class that offered lessons in drawing, painting, and writing. The school's general curriculum included reading, writing, arithmetic, penmanship, oratory, Latin, and astronomy for the white school. For the Native American students, the curriculum included practical arithmetic, reading, spelling, singing, mental arithmetic, geography, and proficiency in English. All the girls were taught knitting, embroidery, crocheting, dressmaking, and some of the arts.

After 1896, the Jesuits determined to leave St. Peter's Mission, and the Ursuline Sisters, in addition to the white and Native American girls from several tribes, took on the boys' education. Mother Philippa Seery is with the boys here. Note the two young lads in a tree.

A group of boys poses in front of a stone building at St. Peter's Mission. They appear to be dressed for an occasion or a performance. This building burned in 1907.

Children at St. Peter's Mission pose for a photograph in and around a hayrack. The children enjoyed outings in the beautiful open country around St. Peter's Mission.

Seven women are pictured at a camp, including Ursuline sisters, novices, and postulants. Picnics and walks in the area around Peter's mission were frequent forms of recreation enjoyed by adults as well as students.

Rev. Mother St. Julien Aubrey was elected the general superior of the Roman Union Ursulines after it was formed in 1900. She had been instrumental in arranging cooperation between three of the monasteries in Europe. This sharing spread to many of the other monasteries, even beyond Europe. In June 6, 1906, she came to America and spent time at St. Peter's Mission.

Mother Amadeus Dunne was the leader of the group of Ursulines who came from Ohio to be with the Native American people in Montana. From the six sisters who came, the number of sisters grew, as did the number of missions served by the sisters. In all, she sent sisters to eight missions across the state during her tenure.

St. Peter's Mission served as the motherhouse for Ursuline sisters in Montana, and many nuns resided and received training here. Pictured are a group of over 20 sisters, including Rev. Mother St. Julien Aubrey, the general superior from Rome (third row, sixth from left), and to her right is Mother Amadeus Dunne, the superior of the Montana missions. In 1908, after fire destroyed some of the buildings at St. Peter's Mission, the sisters considered the wish of Bishop Lenihan that they establish a school in Great Falls. The school was also called Mount Angela Academy and Ursuline Academy. It opened in 1912. The school at St. Peter's continued for the Native American students until 1918 when the large stone building also burned. At that time, the girls transferred to one of the other missions.

Mount Angela Ursuline Academy at St. Peter's was in ruins after a fire destroyed the building in 1918. This second fire at the mission determined the close of St. Peter's Mission altogether. The Caucasian girls who wished to continue with their education moved to the new school, Ursuline Academy in Great Falls. The Native American girls moved to one of the other missions.

A group of sisters and a priest examine the rubble and ruins at St. Peter's Mission. The site at St. Peter's has continued to be a favorite place to visit for many. The country is rugged yet tranquil, and beautiful mountains and grasslands abound. Local community members continue to watch over the mission chapel that still stands at St. Peter's.

Three

URSULINE ACADEMY

The Ursuline Sisters' tradition of spiritual guidance and academic excellence continued in the large academy opened in the nearby city of Great Falls, Montana. Pictured here are Mother Ignatius Casey (standing) and Mother Agnus Dunne (seated at the table) with seven of their students. The academy offered a range of courses and activities for the people of the city and neighboring communities.

The Ursuline Sisters' property surrounding the academy totaled four city blocks, pictured here after 1932. The city gave permission to close First Avenue South between Twenty-third and Twenty-fifth Streets and also Twenty-fourth Street between Second Avenue South and Central Avenue. The front of the building faces north. The gymnasium was erected behind the main building and faces Twenty-third Street. To the east is space for large gardens. Additionally, just on the left edge of the photograph at the corner of Central Avenue and Twenty-fifth Street is the foundation of the College of Great Falls, established in 1932, which remained unfinished due to the Depression.

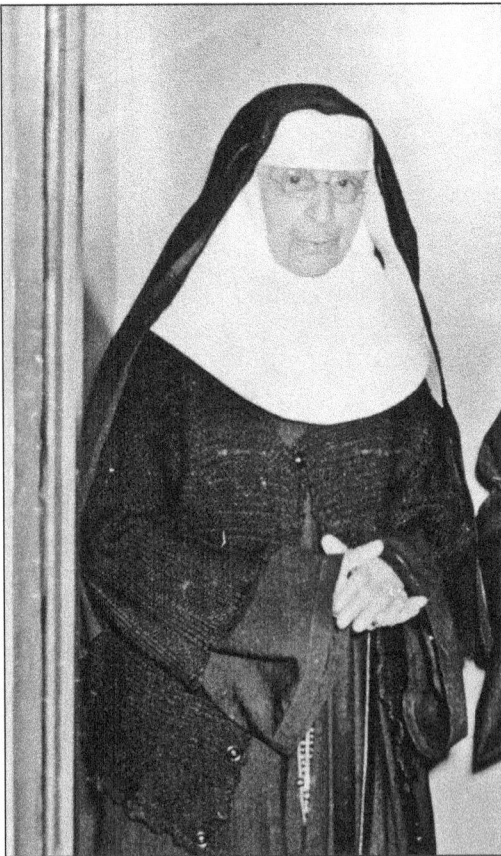

Of the six Ursulines who came to Montana from Toledo, Mother Francis Seibert was the only one to die in Montana. As superior of the Ursuline community in St. Peter's at the time the community moved to Great Falls, she continued as superior during the beginning days of Ursuline Academy. She was responsible for managing the operation of the building as well as planning for the school.

Mother Perpetua Egan came to the Indian missions in Montana from St. Louis. Later, in Great Falls, Mother Francis delegated managing the business affairs to her. One time, when she needed $10,000 to pay the workers, bankers in Great Falls, Butte, and Missoula would not risk a loan. She went to a friend on the Flathead Indian Reservation in Northwestern Montana, Michael Pablo, who gave her the cash with "no interest, no hurry pay back."

Bishop Mathias Lenihan was the first bishop when the Diocese of Great Falls was created. He was influential in opening the school and supportive of the academic progress of the academy throughout his tenure as bishop from 1904 to 1930. Entries in the Ursuline Sisters' annals mark his interest in the location of the campus. He participated in ceremonies and graduations.

Famed local architect George Shanley designed the Ursuline Academy in Great Falls. The contractor was Leighland Kleppe and Company. The 64,000-square-foot building was a significant undertaking that put many local men to work. The building was equipped with modern conveniences, such as plumbing, heating, and electricity.

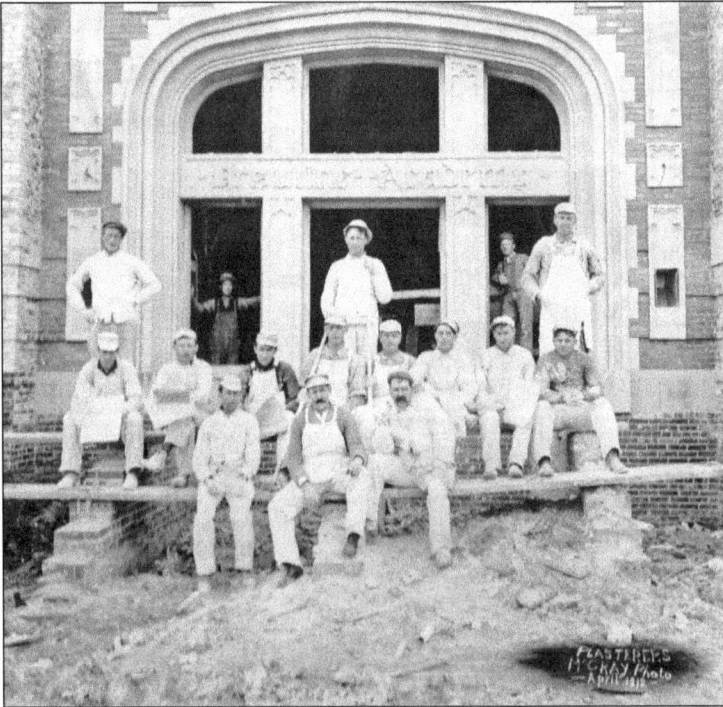

The cornerstone of the building was laid in September 1911, and on September 3, 1912, Mount Angela Academy welcomed the first students, both day students and boarders. Decorative terra-cotta coping and wall ornamentation as well as eight gargoyles atop the building's tower, emulate collegiate Gothic Revival architecture.

In addition to providing an excellent, comprehensive education, the Ursuline Sisters, pictured here, shared in the labor and hardships of the early days. From left to right are (first row) Mother Rose Drapeau; (second row) Mothers Camilla Fouts, Aloysius Bailey, Agnes Dunne, Francis Seibert, and John Unverdorben; (third row) Mothers Loretta Lenehan, Immaculata McLaughlin, unidentified, del Pilar Hatton, Genevieve McBride, Regina Kiernan, Elizabeth Amrhein, and Juliana Kelly.

An August 4, 1912, news clipping heralds, "Splendid New Building Open for Inspection," and it was reported, "from early noon until late in the evening crowds of people visited the academy." A 1912 postcard shows the building around the time of its opening, when it stood almost alone on upper Central Avenue.

As the city grew, so did the need for quality educational facilities. The grand endeavor to establish a substantial academy required vision, leadership, and financial support from several sources. Especially needed was a willingness to take risks. Ursuline sisters worked with the bishop and

local citizens to accomplish these tasks. This photograph was taken from atop Ursuline Academy in its early years. (Courtesy of the History Museum in Great Falls, Montana.)

Throughout the years, the main doors and front entrance have been a place and a symbol of welcome. When Ursuline Academy opened its doors for the first time, the sisters welcomed about 40 boarders, 25 day pupils, and 30 music pupils. These students were registered in the excellent academic programs offered by the sisters.

This 1915 photograph shows children of every school age. They are not in uniform, so the photograph may have been taken on the first days of the school year. There are also some adults, perhaps lay teachers or parents.

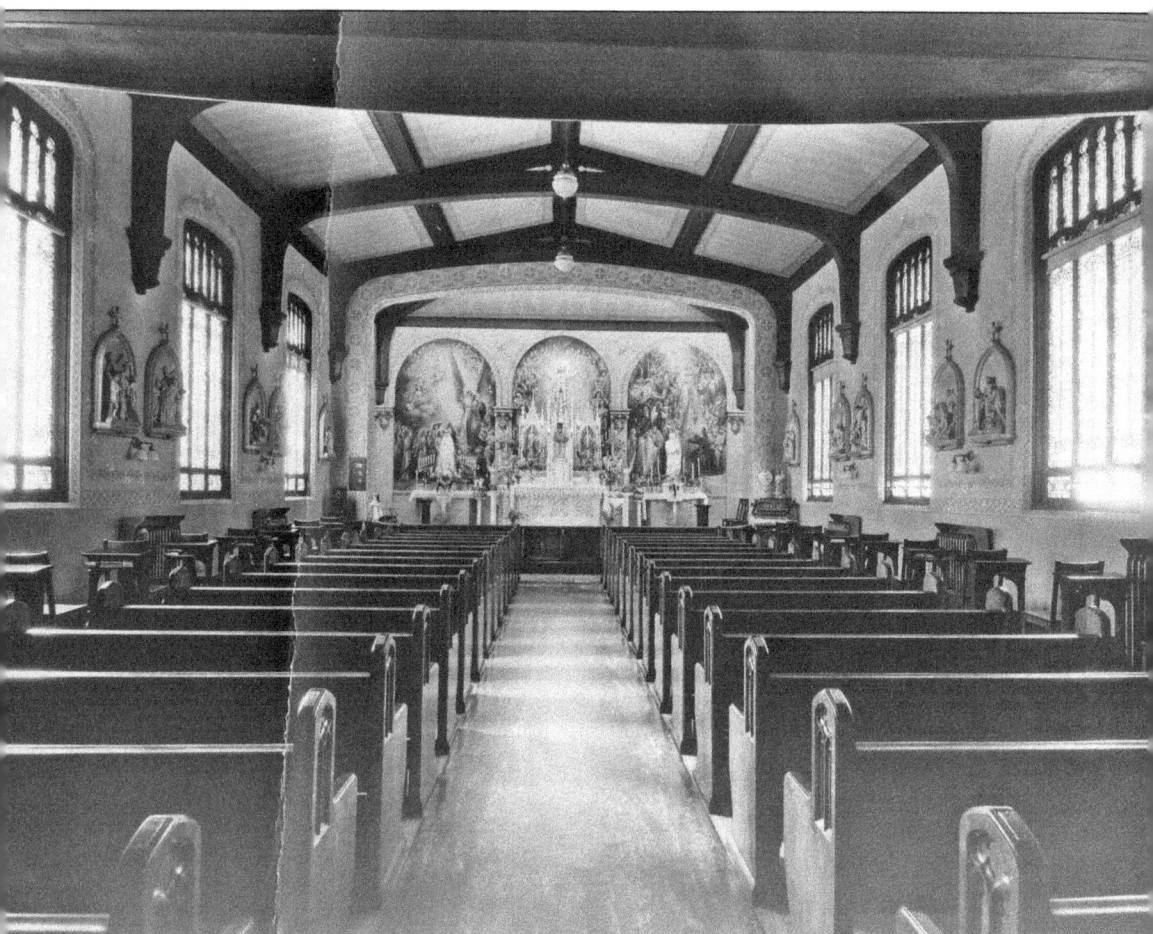

From the earliest time of Ursuline Academy, the chapel was recognized as the center of the life of the Ursuline Sisters, and appreciation of it as a quiet place for prayer was incorporated as part of the spiritual guidance offered the students in the school. The statue of the Sacred Heart above the tabernacle is similar to one placed in every Ursuline chapel by Mother Amadeus Dunne. It and the statues of Mary and Joseph were brought from St. Peter's when the sisters moved to Great Falls. The paintings of St. Angela and St. Ursula, as well as the 14 Stations of the Cross around the walls, provided much opportunity for reflection and prayer. Sisters gathered here several times a day, and students joined them regularly for Mass or Benediction.

Pictured here from left to right are Mothers Mary Reitz, Laurence Reuter, Theodore Levi, and Dolores Helbling. They stand in the wind behind the building. Some of the porches on each floor of the east wing are shown in the photograph. These porches served as entry to a fire escape stairway.

From left to right, Mothers Agnes Dunne, Ignatius Casey, and Lutegarde Jones stand at one corner of the front entrance. These old-timers took time to look over the grounds in front of the academy building. Each one played a significant role in the work of the early days in Great Falls.

The nuns pictured here on the front steps are Mothers Laurence Holland, Augustine Cuff, Rose Whalen, Finbarr Kriener, Agnes Dunne, and Devine Heart Cuff. From the early days in Great Falls, these front steps came to be a favorite place for gathering and taking pictures. Mothers Devine Heart and Augustine, sisters, came to the Montana missions from their home in Philadelphia.

From left to right, Mothers John Fort, Ignatius Casey, Laurence Holland, Cecilia Wiegand, Ursula Marie Walters, and Immaculata McLaughlin stand together in the yard. Mother John came to Montana in 1905 as a French exile at the time of religious unrest in France during the 19th and early 20th century. The others joined the Ursulines after meeting them closer to home in rural Montana and Washington.

Mother Ferdinand Diekhaus was an excellent teacher of students at any level. She taught Latin, logic, psychology, literature, and composition. Born in Germany, she joined the Ursulines in St. Louis and, in addition to Great Falls, served in Ursuline schools in California, Washington, Cuba, and Java (Indonesia).

Mothers Ursula Marie (left) and Antoinette Johnson, sisters, are shown during the years they were living at Ursuline Academy. During their retirement years, they were able to spend time in the same community. Mother Antoinette had spent many of her active years in Alaska among the Eskimo people, whereas Mother Ursula Marie labored long in the music department in Great Falls.

From left to right, Mothers Madeleine Hethernan, Ursula Marie Johnson, Benedict Griffin, Francis Jarboe, Clotilde McBride, and Elisabeth Marie Charvet are looking over a display of children's books on the Life of Christ. Mother Clotilde, a librarian, chose excellent books to help the teachers in all the subject areas. Because the academy encompassed all levels, including junior college, the library housed reference materials appropriate for each level.

Montana Ursulines gathered in Great Falls during vacation for retreats, summer school, or educational meetings. Standing on the front steps from left to right are (first row) Mothers Rita Fleshman, Rose Whelan, Ignatius Casey, Emmanuel Adams, Margaret Mary Brosnan, Augustine Cuff, Stanislaus Maring, and Cecilia Felciano; (second row) Devine Heart Cuff, Xavier Gavigan, Agnes Dunne, Mechtilde Dinndorf, Columba Kirby, Annunciata Dunne, and Laurence Holland.

The campus of Ursuline Academy offered much opportunity for physical activity. The building, lawns, and front walks covered the block facing Central Avenue between Twenty-third and Twenty-fourth Streets. The block east contained a garden, a small utility building, and open space where the foundation for a college building was situated. The two blocks behind between First

and Second Avenues South was a schoolyard for the students. This photograph shows students playing croquet. Others are entertained by a circle game and the maypole. Seesaws and swings are also pictured. There is a covered area where tables and benches could be used for other activities or for lunch. A sister in the background oversees all the activity.

Music was offered from the beginning at Ursuline Academy. Coursework included options for study in a stringed instrument and voice. In this early image, the students of the stringed orchestra pose with their instruments in the parlor. The pictures that hang on the wall behind them continue to adorn the walls of the building today.

The academy's Spanish Club poses for a photograph during the 1920–1921 academic year. The club was one of many groups offered to the students. Other opportunities included becoming a member of the student council or staff for the official yearbook, *The Link*. Students could also join clubs, including the Mission Club, Sodality, or the Don Bosco Club.

Six young women are busy in the chemistry lab at Ursuline Academy.

This photograph shows a biology class in 1940. Ursuline Academy offered biology and advanced sciences. The uniform had changed from earlier years, when a bolo tie and vest were worn.

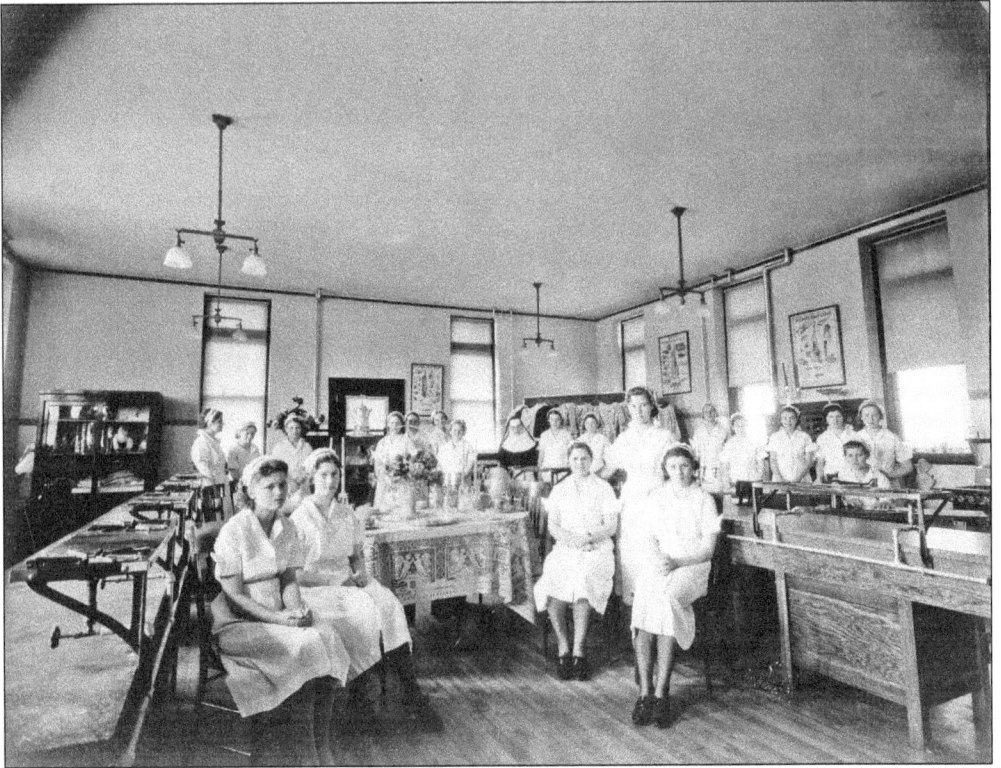

The home economics class is gathered for what seems to be an end-of-the-year evaluation. Note that the tables are equipped with gas lines and burners for cooking. A small but elaborate tea table is set. Student sewing projects hang in the back of the room near an Ursuline sister.

Reading, writing, and arithmetic were mastered before advanced coursework began. In this upper-level class in logic, students in the early 1940s demonstrate the value of the correct use of a syllogism.

Opportunity for commercial training was available to Ursuline students. Here, young women focus on typing and transcribing.

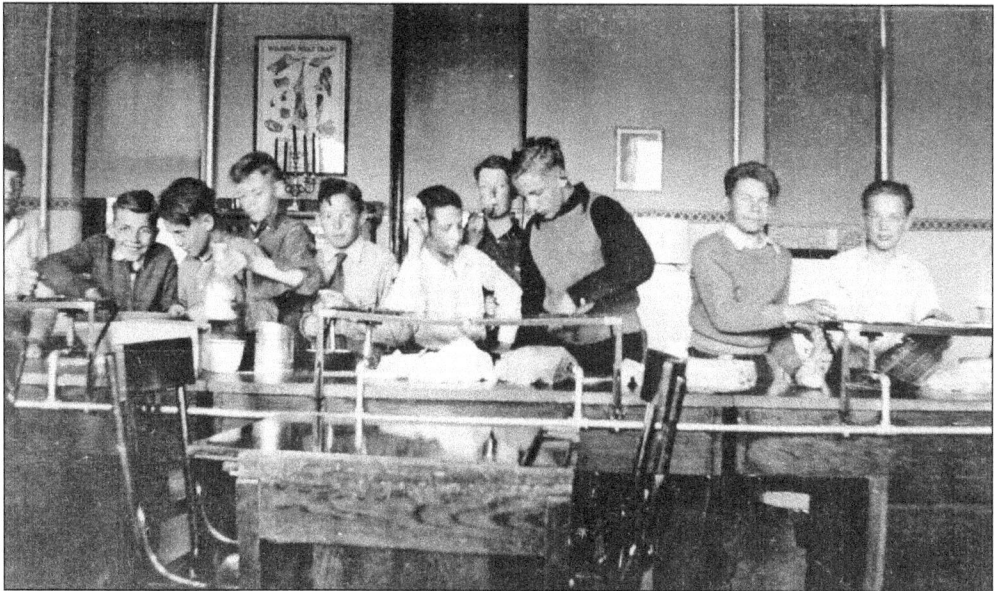

Boys attended Ursuline Academy from the beginning, though they did not board until an addition to the gymnasium was built in 1925. Throughout the history of Ursuline, academy boys were accepted as day students at every level. In this photograph, a class of boys enjoys a cooking lesson, several of them with ingredients in hand.

The gymnasium was built in 1925. When more classroom space was needed, this building replaced the original gym at the east end of the main building. The new gymnasium boasted a hardwood floor, brand-new backboards with hoops, and bleachers for family and spectators. All types of sports were played in the new facility. The main door faced Twenty-third Street.

The fourth- and fifth-grade classes pose in this early 1930s photograph. The girls wore similar uniforms with long ties. Throughout the life of the school, the girls wore uniforms but the boys did not. Pictured here, the west entrance to the building and the west stairs were the ones to be used by students. Francis Jenks is named on the back of the photograph.

Members of the class of 1930 stand in a line against the wall outside their dining room. Class pictures were common and sometimes served as features in the official school yearbook, *The Link*. At this period, there were not many pictures in a yearbook. It was a student production and contained samples of their writings, a calendar of their activities, and an update on alumnae.

In 1932, the faculty consisted mostly of Ursuline sisters. Pictured from left to right are (first row) Mothers Alphonsus Devitt, Loyola Meneger, Agnes Dunne, Monsignor John Regan, unidentified, Mothers Ignatius Casey, Monica Reardon, and Clotilde McBride; (second row) Mother Amata Marie McNaught, Mother Helen McVee, Mother Angela Griffin, unidentified, Dorris King, unidentified, Mother James McLaughlin, Mother Raphael Schweida, and Mother Anne Marie Fouts.

The original design of the building called for a gymnasium at the east end with the floor lower than the main hall. There was a large, open space for exercise drills. A basketball hoop and a piano are also be seen in the photograph. When the separate gymnasium was built in 1925, the floor was raised in this area, and it was modified to contain three classrooms.

The 1923, basketball team, from left to right, included (first row) Gladys Heaney, Letty Devereaux, Genevieve Van de Putte, Mary Regan, and Susan Goldschmidt; (second row) Evelyn Church and coach Margaret McBride. Margaret McBride became an Ursuline as Mother Genevieve McBride.

A group of students pose with Mother Elizabeth Amrhein. She came to Montana from Boston in 1892 as a missionary. Well known throughout the state for her talent in music, languages, and fine arts, she continued this work when the community moved from St. Peter's to Great Falls. She held a master's degree and was a member of the first college faculty. She was also active in student activities such as drama productions and public-speaking contests. It was important that the young ladies be able to able to present themselves well. This photograph was taken after 1925; note the new gymnasium in the background.

A world map is seen behind Mother Margaret Mary Brosnan as she conducts a history class. One of the early graduates of Ursuline Academy, she also graduated from the Ursuline College of New Rochelle in New York. She taught many years at the academy and was one of the first faculty of Central Catholic High School. From 1932 until 1938, she was superior of the Ursuline Western Province.

The calendar on the wall dates this image to February 1947. Msgr. Francis J. Saksa, the chancellor of the Diocese of Great Falls, taught a course in religion. He was the resident chaplain at Ursuline Academy and presided over liturgical services for the sisters as well as the students.

Members of the boys' basketball team at Ursuline Academy are pictured here around 1940. The team members from left to right are Pat Egan, John Boland, Leroy Marxer, Joe Kappas, and Jack Galt.

Ursuline Academy journalists work in the library in the early 1940s. An array of reference books and other literary works line the shelves, and two students sit at typewriters. Between the general library, seen here, and the special reference library, the book collection totaled over 12,000 volumes.

Delegates to a Sodality meeting in Spokane pose for a photograph. The Sodality is a religious activity. On Sunday, the hour from 9:00 to 10:00 a.m. is spent in honor of Mary. Members either chant the Office of the Blessed Virgin or recite the rosary. On the first Sunday, they attend Mass and receive Communion as a body. The aim of the Sodality is to inspire greater devotion to Mary.

A special meal is enjoyed in the girls' recreation room in the early 1940s. Preparation for and conduct at such an occasion were included as part of the training in the home economics course.

Dances were annual affairs at Ursuline Academy. This photograph shows the 1937 junior prom in the school gymnasium, which has been elaborately decorated for the occasion.

Ten students pose for a photograph in the grand entryway of Ursuline Academy. Their formal dress indicates preparation for a musical concert. The entryway was reserved for special occasions, including opportunities for photographs. It featured a marble staircase. This group, assisted by the high school chorus, presented the operetta *Jeanne D'Arc*. Principal roles were filled by members of the Glee Club.

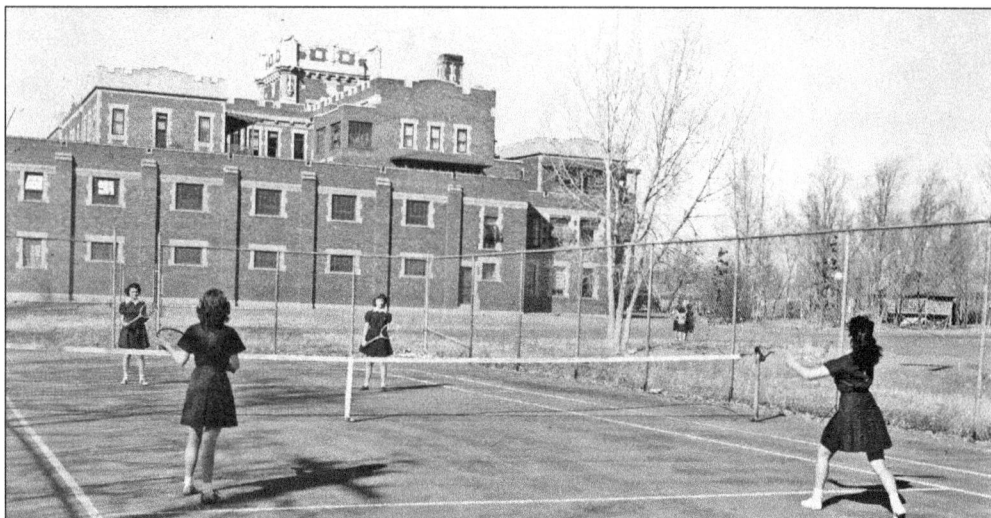

A full tennis court was located behind the gymnasium to the south of the building. Here, four students with rackets participate in a match. Note that there are only two spectators.

This photograph shows a student about to serve the volleyball during a physical education class in 1942. The students are in their gymnasium uniforms, and there is an excellent view of the gymnasium, showing the playing floor and bleachers. Score was kept on the blackboard shown.

High school students process throughout the building while carrying lighted candles and singing Christmas carols. Here, they are coming down the west stairs, used by the students; the stairs on the east end were reserved for the sisters.

This room contained a reference library. The rare and valuable books are part of the collection that came to Montana with Mother Angela Lincoln. These books brought the total at the school library to nearly 12,000 volumes.

The school library moved over time. This photograph is of the second room that was used for the library. Located on the third floor across from the chapel, it later became a kindergarten classroom. The two tables for research or work in the library had previously been pianos.

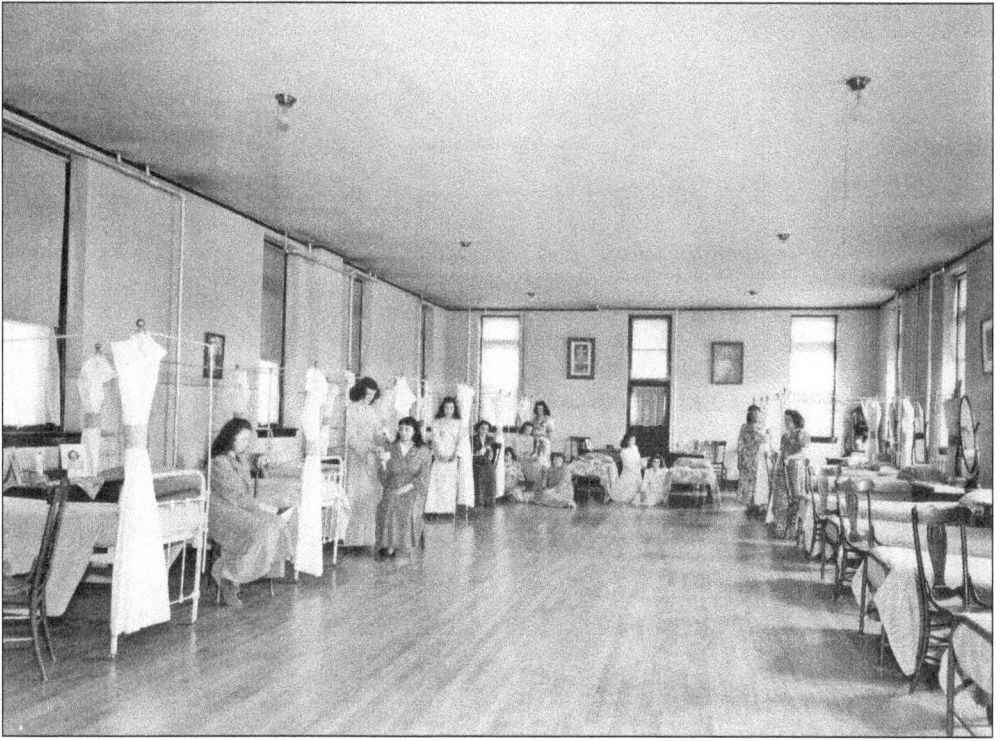

Two large rooms on the second floor provided dormitories for the boarding students, separated according to age. Each bed had a curtain for privacy and very simple furnishings. Each girl's clothes and other belongings were kept in a locker in the entry to the dormitory. Later, one of the dormitories was converted into the third location for the library.

Three students are pictured in a private boarding room at Ursuline Academy. In addition to living in a dormitory, a student could choose a private room. In the early days, there were many boarding students. Later, as travel became easier, more girls became day students.

Between the academy building and the play yards and to the east of the gymnasium is a small, grassy park. In the center of the park is a grotto of Our Lady. Over the years, it has been a place of devotion for nuns, students, and visitors to Ursuline.

Throughout its history, Ursuline Academy has encouraged devotion to Christ's Mother Mary. Boarding students were invited to belong to the Sodality of Mary, and on special feast days, ceremonies were held in the chapel and outside at the grotto. Note the banner carried in procession. Father John Regan leads the prayer at the grotto.

The students, particularly members of the Sodality, participated in some of the prayers said by the sisters. The Little Office of the Blessed Virgin was one similar to the Devine Office recited daily by priests. This photograph may show a practice for some later ceremony. The pipe organ in the balcony is visible, as is the communion rail with the cloth ready to cover the top during Mass. Such a cloth ceased to be used in the 1950s, and now, communion rails are in place only as historical objects. The pipe organ was also replaced when it became too difficult manage.

The cornerstone of the College of Great Falls was laid east of the academy near Twenty-fifth Street. The college was a joint venture of the Sisters of Providence and the Ursulines under the direction of the bishop of Great Falls. Until this time in 1932, there was no educational opportunity in Great Falls beyond high school. Due to economic conditions of the time, the building was not completed.

Sr. Genevieve McBride, OSU, a scholar and an educator, was appointed the first dean of the College of Great Falls. Classes were held at Ursuline Academy in the Green Parlor. As enrollment increased and curriculum expanded, classes continued both at the academy and near the hospital a few blocks away. The Sisters of Providence have since expanded the college into a university.

College students visit on the steps at the northeast entrance to Ursuline Academy. In 1932, the door pictured here was marked with "Great Falls College" to honor the college students.

Over the decades, Ursuline Academy provided quality Catholic education to children of Great Falls and the surrounding area. The children, parents, alumni, and members of organizations were all able to share in the expertise and the dedication of the Ursuline Sisters and their fellow educators.

Four

SPECIAL PROGRAMS AND OUTREACH

When the new parish school was established in 1945 at Our Lady of Lourdes, in order to teach there, Ursuline sisters commuted from the academy daily. Pictured from left to right as they prepare to leave for the day are Mothers Andre Kuhry, Elisabeth Marie Charvet, Basil Crawley, and Immaculata McLaughlin.

When the sisters began at Our Lady of Lourdes, only the church building was completed. Classes were for only a few grades and conducted in the church basement. The school, shown on the right of the photograph, came later as a result of much labor and struggle by the parishioners.

Mother Madeleine Hethernan celebrates with her eighth-grade graduates at Our Lady of Lourdes. By 1950, all eight grades made up the school population, and the school building had been added to the church. In 1968, a separate community of Ursuline sisters was created, and they moved from the academy to a home near the school.

The Ursuline Sisters, along with dedicated volunteers, arranged to provide religious education classes to the Catholic students at the Montana Deaf and Blind School. Mothers Mechtilde Dindorf and Andre Kuhry were devoted to this ministry. The school was a state institution, and many of the activities were held at either Holy Family or Our Lady of Lourdes Parish. Pictured here are a few students at Our Lady of Lourdes.

In addition to outreach to parishes and organizations, when the opportunity presented itself, the sisters shared among the schools where they taught. Mother Theodore Levi directed a boys' choir in several schools. Pictured are boys who have gathered to perform on the stage at Ursuline Academy. Mother Theodore was a favored teacher in Anaconda. When moved to Great Falls, she worked with students in Ursuline Academy and Our Lady of Lourdes.

The Ursuline Sisters have a large school in Caracas, Venezuela, where the spoken language is Spanish. The faculty, as well as students, wanted to learn more English. This presented another opportunity for sisters in Great Falls at Ursuline Academy to reach out. Mother Angela Griffin is pictured with students she taught in Caracas. The desire to spread the word of God and teach in other parts of the world was not uncommon in those women associated with Ursuline Academy. For example, Mother Theophane Westerman graduated from Ursuline Academy in 1925. After she joined the order, she volunteered for the missions and was sent to Siam (Thailand), where she taught school and worked with the Thai people for most of her adult life. Ursulines continue to be active outside of Europe and the United States in missions across the world.

During a few weeks in the summer when academy students had gone home, some sisters would go to the rural parishes for two weeks to teach religion and prepare children for First Communion. Here, a group of vacation school students in Hot Springs, Montana, pose with Rev. Father Mellady and two Ursuline sisters, Mother Teresa Abair and unidentified. This image was taken during the summer of 1933 in Hot Springs.

This photograph was taken in 1946 in Plains, Montana, where children pose with Mothers Andre Kuhry and Clement Marie Schmieder. First Communion was an occasion to wear their very best, and girls usually wore a white veil. The OSU's efforts to provide religious instruction for Montana residents reached far beyond their established schools, as with many summer religious education programs.

In the 1930s, sisters went to the Rocky Boy Indian Reservation to help with the summer religion program. In class with the large group of students are the two Menager sisters, Mothers Loyola and Incarnation. Though the Ursuline Sisters did not operate a day school at Rocky Boy, they felt it was important to offer religious training through summer courses for the residents there.

Holy Family, a mission school for the Blackfeet children, was forced to close in 1941 due to a lack of funding. Sisters then went to help with religious education and prepare children to receive their First Communion during Vacation School each summer. Pictured here in 1947, Children in the class pose in front of the church with Fr. E.E. Mallman, Jesuit pastor of the church at Holy Family, and Ursuline sister Mother Charvet.

From the beginning, laywomen in the community supported Ursuline Academy. They formed a Ursuline Academy Ladies Auxiliary to raise funds for a scholarship and provide for many other needs they recognized. Activities included such things as card parties and an annual tea. As early as 1915, they supplied all the students' textbooks. In the image above, dated December 7, 1946, Penny McBride, a charter member, is seated with officers of the auxiliary during a special event. At left, Mother Genevieve McBride poses with auxiliary members at an annual Christmas tea. The Ursuline auxiliary had constitutions and bylaws that stated their purpose, which included study of religious, civic, social, educational, and philanthropic subjects. According to archival research, they wrote letters to members of congress regarding votes to be taken when needed.

The Ursuline auxiliary and the alumni of Ursuline Academy often participated together in activities to support the academy. Above, Mothers Ursula Marie Johnson (left) and Angela Griffin visit in the parlor after one such activity. Parents of the sisters also made up an active group of supporters for the school. Frances Porter (left) and Catherine Lorang both had daughters who were Ursulines. They are pictured below visiting with, from left to right, Mothers Francis Xavier Porter, Helen McVee, and James McLaughlin.

Graduation day at Ursuline Academy is shown in these two images. The graduation ceremony took place on the front steps, and the celebration of congratulation moved to the front lawn. These pictures show the front of the building and the lawn in the early history of the school.

In 1962, Ursuline Academy was 50 years old. The Ursuline Sisters had the opportunity to meet changing needs through many programs. These ranged from academic and cultural opportunities offered through their academy to outreach in local parish schools and beyond. During the second part of the century, the high school at Ursuline had joined with two others to become Central Catholic School. Ursulines were involved there as faculty members, and Ursuline Academy continued to serve as an elementary school. Pictured here is the planning committee for Ursuline Academy's Golden Jubilee. From left to right, they are Mother Mary Laurence Reuter, unidentified, Mother Angela Griffin, Helen McNaught Parchens, and Patrick Egan.

During the summer months, Ursuline Academy was the location for retreats and conferences for the Diocese of Great Falls. For several years, the annual retreat for the priests of the diocese was held at the academy. Pictured is the group of mostly priests and sisters who participated in diocesan retreat programs. His Excellency Edwin V. O'Hara, a bishop during the 1930s, is in the center of the first row.

Ursuline Academy long served as the meeting place for youth groups such as the Girl Scouts of America. Pictured at the grotto of the Blessed Virgin Mary with Rev. Mother Lawrence Reuter, is a group of Scouts of all ages. Their leader, Leonida Hagan gives rose bushes to Mother Mary Laurence Reuter. Also pictured is Mother Mary Rose Drapeau, who oversaw planting the roses.

Many First Communions were celebrated over the years at Ursuline Academy, including this class photographed on the front steps in the early years. Children receive First Communion after religious training, which was offered either as part of the curriculum during the school year or at the academy (to children who attended public schools during the academic year) during a special religion program in the summer.

The chapel is adorned simply by Mother Raphael's murals in the background, statues of Mary and Joseph on either side of the altar, and the stained-glass windows. Pictured here is Benediction, probably at the close of a retreat. Throughout the history of the Ursuline Sisters in Great Falls, retreats were offered for laypeople as well as students.

While sharing the ministry of Catholic education with some very dedicated and talented laypersons, the sisters grew to love and rely on them. These coworkers were classroom teachers, music instructors, maintenance workers, groundskeepers, and especially cooks that were essential to the operation of the school. This c. 1950 photograph shows Betty Boyd (left) and her helper Sr. Stella O'Driscoll. At the beginning of the school in 1912, the sisters employed only a few laywomen as faculty in the school to provide the needed expertise in particular academic disciplines. Some of these dedicated persons over the years were Doris King (business), Clara Grunenfelder (science), Theodor and Sophie Lemba (instrumental music), and A. Keyes (vocal). During World War II, through the National Catholic Welfare Council, the Ursuline Sisters received displaced persons from Europe. Pictured below are pianists Theodor Lemba (left) and his wife, Sophie Lemba, who came to live at Ursuline Academy from Europe.

A service man from the 7th Ferry Command visits with children at Ursuline Academy. He demonstrates a jeep like the ones the children purchased as part of a nationwide school campaign to support the war effort. Happy children hold war bonds and stamps that were sold during the lunch hour.

A paper drive was another way that Ursuline Academy students showed patriotism during World War II. High school classes competed to see who could collect the most paper for recycling. During the 1943 local scrap drive, Ursuline students collected more than 3,000 pounds. The gymnasium took on a special look and use.

Music was an integral part of Ursuline Academy's curriculum, and from the beginning, the girls were coached in glee clubs. Those with special talent were able to participate in advanced chorus, and there was a choir in which interested students learned the religious music for liturgical services. The Ursuline Academy Glee Club performed regularly. This was partly for entertainment and partly to give the students practice in appearing in front of the public. The club had monthly recitals in the auditorium for the school. The members entertained at the Ursuline auxiliary functions and for various other occasions. The glee club was much in demand. In the early days, Mother Elizabeth Amrhein or Mother Incarnation Meneger directed the vocal groups. Later, it was Mother Theodore Levi with Prof. R.A. Keyes. The professor also directed individual students in giving vocal concerts. This photograph shows the glee club at the Christmas tea.

This group of young performers participated in Ursuline Academy's May Festival in 1954. It was the custom for students to entertain their parents and friends each spring.

The physical education program included lessons in ballet. Physical fitness took on new significance in 1943 due in part to the war effort. Calisthenics and military drill were part of the program, as were kickball, folk dancing, basketball, softball, and track. Interclass competition was well organized, and each year, a school basketball team had the opportunity to play another school.

Mother Raphael Schweda produced numerous works of art and taught art at Ursuline Academy for over 50 years. Classically trained as a child in Europe, she went on to achieve a master's degree in fine arts from the University of Notre Dame. Mother Raphael entered the OSU at St. Peter's Mission in 1912. When the Ursuline community was moved to Great Falls, she taught art at the academy.

Mother Raphael taught art in many mediums at Ursuline Academy. Instruction included watercolor and oil painting, sculpture, and other relief projects.

Students in the academy look at Mother Raphael's painting in the main hall on the second floor. The large paintings at the main entrance testify to Ursuline personnel's key religious beliefs and to their appreciation of fine art. The central painting depicts Jesus on a throne as Christ the King. The face of the figure of Christ seems to shift as the viewer moves along the hall. The paintings on one side show the Annunciation, when the Angel Gabriel appeared to Mary to tell her that God had chosen her to become the mother of his son Jesus, and on the other side, the Resurrection shows Christ just as he has risen from the tomb.

The high school students present *Shepherd of His Flock* to Bishop William Condon during his first visit to Ursuline Academy. Mother Clotilde McBride worked on staging and costumes, and Mother Immaculata Harley directed the play. Drama was an important art form offered at Ursuline Academy over the years. It was one way the school was able to reach out to share with the larger Great Falls community.

In this 1951 Christmas play, students portray the birth of Jesus in the manger with the city of Bethlehem in the background. There were many presentations directed by sisters and performed by students during various seasons of the year. Mother Raphael painted many of the backdrops and made costumes for the plays.

Art and drama played a very important part in Ursuline education. In 1940, Mothers Benedict Griffin and Amata Marie McNaught directed grade school students in the operetta *Hansel and Gretel*, as seen above. Lead roles were played by members of the eighth grade, including, from left to right, John Henen, Richard Boland, Eugene Eagan, Donald Topel, Mary Rice, Richard Hall, Betty Jo Trerise, Mary Jean Fogerty, and Jean Peiton. In 1937 and 1938, students preformed *The Court of King Arthur*, pictured below. The older students, including those in college, participated in some very elaborate plays. These were presented annually during Lent at the academy, off campus at the Heisey, or at another stage in the town. Mother Raphael Schweda took care of building the sets, making the costumes, and directing the performances.

Over the years, the Ursuline Sisters of Great Falls embraced St. Angela's vision to adapt to the ever-changing needs of the world. Their work in Great Falls and the surrounding area provided educational and cultural opportunities to many individuals over the decades they served there. The educational and personal foundations laid through these efforts continue to benefit the community to this day.

Five

TRANSITION

In 1950, Ursuline Academy graduated its last high school class. The academy merged with St. Thomas and St. Mary to form a diocesan high school, Central Catholic High School; however, the sisters continued to provide elementary classes in the academy building, with the academic and cultural opportunities typical of Ursuline. Pictured is a group of junior high students during a retreat.

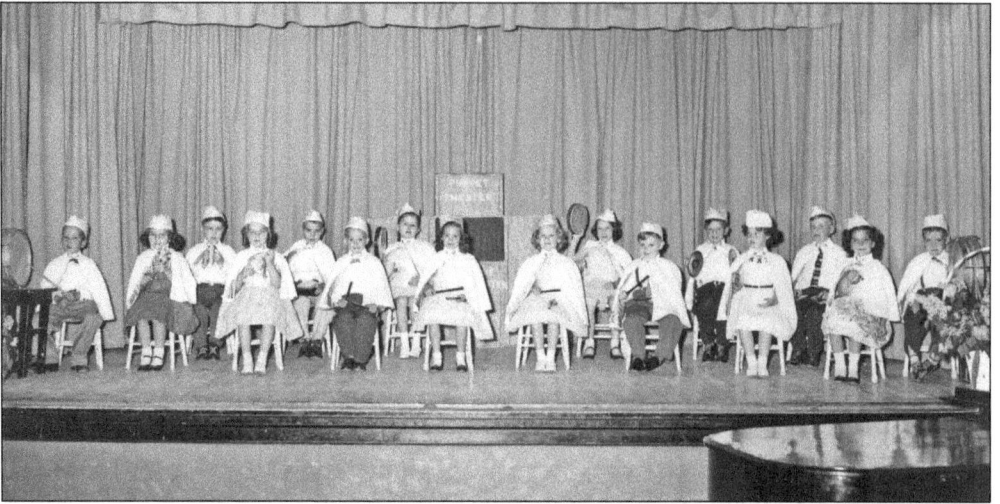

A rhythm band at Ursuline Academy was important for the younger children. Instruments included tambourines, brass cymbals, hand drums, clavicles, blocks, and metal triangles, among others. A sister would have accompanied the students on the piano. The photograph shows the band in uniform on the stage of Ursuline Academy.

A grade school band at Ursuline Academy was organized and directed by Sr. Dolores Helbling. In this photograph, the band performs in the gymnasium as parents and other supporters and spectators sit in the bleachers above. In addition to teaching a class and practicing with the band, Sister Dolores gave students who needed help lessons on a variety of instruments.

Music instruction continued to be offered to grade school children at Ursuline Academy. In this 1952 photograph, the band breaks during a performance in the gymnasium. There was a growing high school band at Central Catholic High School that included former Ursuline students. The director of that band appreciated the beginner's band and the instruction in music students had received at Ursuline. Members of the general public and high school–aged students continued to frequent the academy for private instruction in various types of music. This particular performance and resulting image was captured in the gymnasium though the Ursuline Academy auditorium. With its excellent acoustics, the space continues to be a place for students and adults to perform.

After Ursuline High School merged with other schools in Great Falls to form Central Catholic High School, Ursuline Grade School continued at the academy under the name of Holy Family until 1966. Eventually, Holy Family School moved to the location next to the parish church. For a time, the Ursuline Sisters who taught in that school lived in a convent next to the school and church. In the photograph above, Sr. Clement Maria Schmieder's sixth-grade class stands on the stage of the auditorium. Below, children in Sr. Mary Francis Jaboe's third-grade class sits for their 1954 class photograph.

For over 60 years, hundreds of students attended the grade school program offered at the academy by the Ursuline Sisters. After 1950, eighth-grade graduates either transferred to Central Catholic High School or enrolled at Great Falls High School. Mother Mary Benedicta Callan is seen in the photograph above with her fifth-grade class in 1957. In the photograph below, Sr. Daniel Ryan appears with her kindergarten class. Kindergarten remained active at the academy for years. A preschool program continues to offer a sound educational foundation in a Christian environment for children nearly 100 years later.

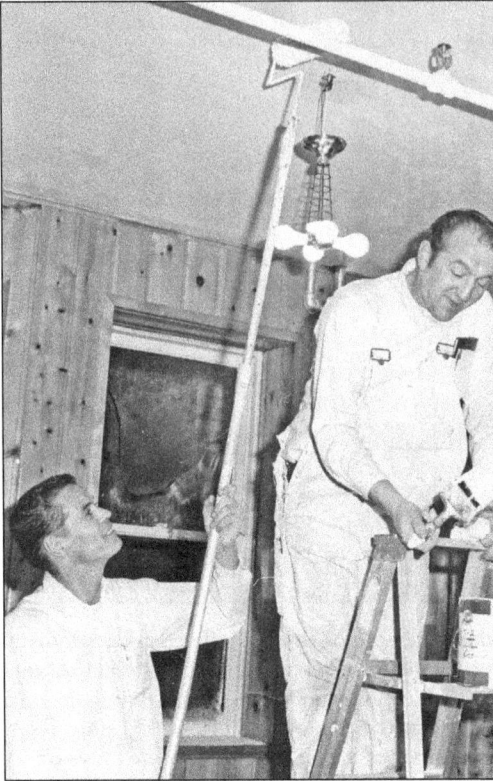

The Ursuline Academy has many rooms of classroom size. Preparing for the transfer from an academy to a full-time retreat center, sisters and generous volunteers worked diligently to prepare parts of the building. During the conversion, the two student dining rooms were adapted to a single room. Devoted volunteers helped take down two partitions, worked to patch the walls, and did a great deal of painting. New blinds were provided for the windows. A partition was installed in the remade dining room to provide for multiple uses when needed. Pictured are some of the workers and a few of the sisters admiring their efforts.

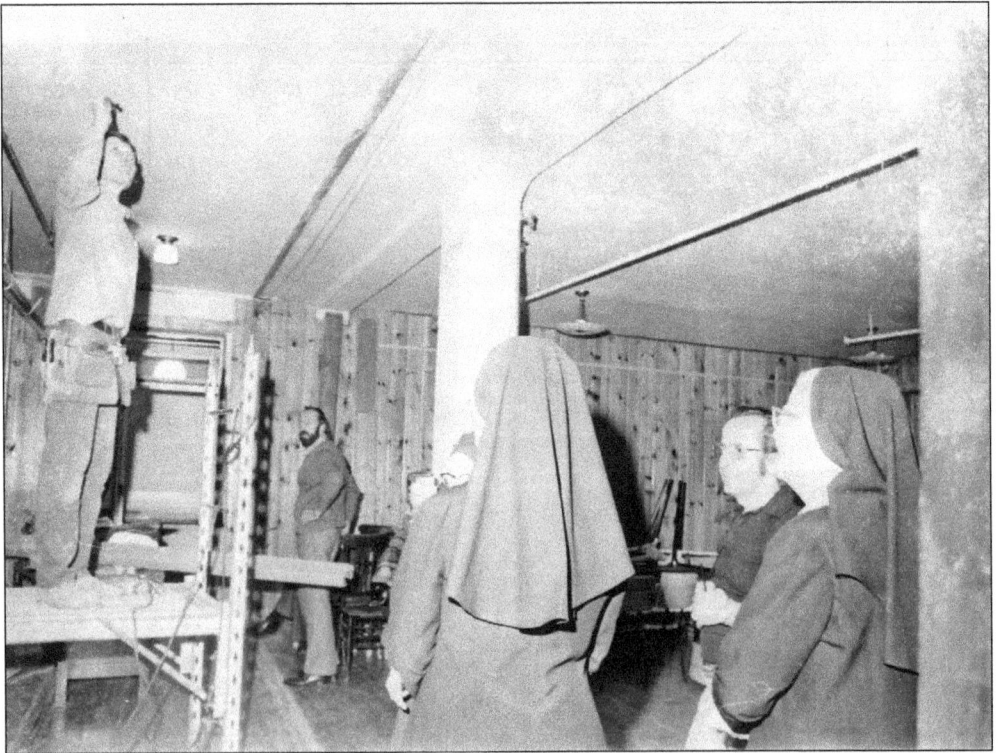

During renovations in 1971, the high school girls' recreation room was made into a conference room. At right, Sr. Dolores Helbling is pictured on a ladder during renovations, assisted by volunteers. The lockers around the walls were removed (except those on the short east wall), the floor was carpeted, and a double door on the north side of the room was opened. Below, Al Harokins breaks through a wall to provide better access from the stairway and the lower hall to what is now known as Lounge One.

The sisters held various activities in the newly renovated Pine Dining Room, ranging from breakfasts to galas. Planning for some further use of this room are, from left to right, Sr. Angela Griffin, Evelyn Broquist, Sr. Benedict Griffin, Sr. Monica Reardon, Sr. Mary Laurence Reuter, and Sr. Athanasius Stevens. This photograph was taken during the transitional years of Ursuline in Great Falls. The sisters wear modified habits. The habit changed from the traditional Ursuline habit after Vatican II and became further modified over the years. Though the habit is no longer worn, Ursuline sisters continue to wear a crucifix and ring.

In 1979, the sisters reached out to meet community members at a People to People picnic at Ryan Dam Park northwest of Great Falls. As the mission of the sisters was transferring from primarily education of youth, adapting to new needs, and new groups of people, they joined in the good works being done by other groups.

The Ursuline Community of Great Falls in the 1980s was composed of sisters, from left to right, (first row) Angela Griffin and Benedict Griffin; (second row) Marian Lorang, Celine Lorang, Andre Kurhy, Marion McCrickard, and Frances Marxer; (third row) Bernadette Charvet, Therese Reily, and Rita Kohut; (fourth row) Florence Copp, Antoinette Johnson, Marietta Devine, and Laurence Reuter, and Daniel Ryan.

Records from each of the eight missions where the Ursuline Sisters served in Montana, beginning in 1884, have been collected and preserved in the archives at Ursuline Centre. These records include journals, letters, photographs, files on individual sisters, and student papers. Pictured is Mother Elisabeth Marie Charvet, the archivist who began sorting the materials that came from the other Ursuline houses.

As records and materials accumulated in the archives, better shelving and acid free boxes were obtained. Julianne Ruby took over as archivist and continued the work of organizing and providing information.

Mother Genevieve McBride examines a beaded belt in the Ursuline collection of ethnographic materials. Mother Genevieve was a scholar and a historian. Her list of accomplishments goes beyond her Ursuline ministry and includes her position as the first dean of the College of Great Falls in 1932. In 1974, her book on St. Peter's Mission, *The Bird Tail*, was published. Her account drew on letters, diaries, annals, and records housed in Ursuline Archives.

The Heritage Museum houses the Ursuline collection of over 200 Native American cultural materials. Most of the collection is from the Northern Plains and includes examples from Crow, Northern Cheyenne, Salish, Kootenai, Cree, and Chippewa people. These were given to and collected by the sisters as they lived among the people at the different missions.

In 2000, Mother Colette Lignon, Ursuline superior general from Rome, poses with sisters of the Great Falls community. Such special visits occurred every six years. Pictured from left to right are Sisters (first row) Angela Griffin and Daniel Ryan; (second row) Helen Rose Kaszubowski, Antoinette Johnson, Carolina Gomez del Valle, Mother Superior Colette Lignon, Elisabeth Marie Charvet, and Ursula Marie Johnson.

Sisters Daniel Ryan (left) and James McLaughlin spend time together in this 1990s photograph. Many retired sisters came to the convent in Great Falls in their later years and shared companionship and time in prayer. Some of the sisters were originally from Great Falls, and others returned after teaching in one or other Ursuline schools.

Especially during their later years, the sisters took time to enjoy an outing, such as a picnic. Many enjoyed being in the mountains or just out in the country, and friends were generous in sharing their property with the sisters. Here, they wait for a ride while holding a sack lunch.

At the Gates of the Mountains on the Missouri River, Sisters Jean Hopman, unidentified, Andre Kuhry, Daniel Ryan, David Hartse, unidentified, and Elisabeth Marie Charvet are getting ready for a boat tour.

From early on, the Ursuline Sisters of Great Falls were joined by laypersons recognized for their devotion and support of the Ursuline ministry; they were referred to as "associates." On January 27, 1996, a reception of new Ursuline associates was held. From left to right are (first row) Beverly Simons, Sr. Helen Rose, and Janis Tholen; (second row) Lillian Grandade, Richard Terra, Joann Evans, unidentified, and Joyce Jewette; (third row) LaVern McFadden, Margaret Walsh, Calvin Ruby, and Julianne Ruby.

The Peace Pole was a gift from the Jubilee Book Club, one of many small groups that have been meeting at Ursuline. The marker reads, "May Peace Prevail on Earth," transcribed in four different languages. Peace is a message embodied by Ursuline sisters' ministry across the world. The pole is on the front east corner of the building. Other small prayer groups meet regularly and enjoy the tranquility of Ursuline Centre.

Between 1970 and 1990, the Ursuline Sisters managed and operated the retreat center with the help of some volunteers. In 1991, they hired the first lay director, Harry Tholen, who had attended the academy as a boy and was one of the most generous volunteers. Pictured in the second row is Gov. Marc Racicot (left) and Harry Tholen.

Over the years, the number of laypersons involved with Ursuline sisters grew as the ministry expanded. A few of the longtime employees pictured from left to right are Cindy Gordon, Silvia Borchert, Sr. Daniel Ryan, and Bonnie Cartwright. Cartwright served as caregiver for the infirm sisters, while Borchert, assisted by Gordon, managed the kitchen for many years. Dozens of people from the community not mentioned in this book have worked with Ursuline sisters during the century they served in Great Falls.

In keeping with the history of providing retreats for students and adults, some of the retired sisters continued to direct an occasional retreat. Pictured is Sr. Helen Rose Kaszubowski with a class from St. Andrew in Helena, Montana, as they prepare to leave after a retreat at Ursuline Centre in April 2000.

One program long valued by Ursuline is the Cum Christo, an ecumenical retreat experience of renewal and spiritual growth. In order to keep up the spirit of the Cum Christo experience, participants have the opportunity to come together weekly for prayer and sharing, known as an Ultreya. Pictured is an Ultreya meeting in 1998 in one of Ursuline's renovated large meeting rooms.

The Montana Association of Churches (MAC) has been meeting at Ursuline Academy for many years. Founded in 1973, the association is made up of leaders from area churches and meets annually. Ursuline sister Marietta Devine, superior of the Ursulines in Great Falls, was an active member of MAC. In 1987, she was named president of the organization.

In keeping with the Ursuline Sisters' history of missionary life in Montana, an annual program called the North American Ursuline Experience is offered to give others the opportunity to experience some of what the early missionaries lived. The inspiration for such a program comes from the book *Lady Blackrobes* by Sr. Irene Mahoney, OSU. Ursuline sisters from around the country pose at the back of the building. From left to right are Sr. Louis Marie Carter, Sr. Francis Porter, Harry Tholen (director of Ursuline Centre), Sr. Marie William Blyth, Sr. Margie Efkeman, Sr. Barbard Niemans, and Sr. Patricia Meisner in the summer of 2008.

Participants in the Elderhostel or Road Scholar program offered by Ursuline Retreat and Conference Centre pose on deck on the east side of the building. This program has become a tradition and is offered once or twice during the summer for a week, during which there are three classes and field trips each day. Topics include artist Charles Russell, Plains Indian culture, and the Lewis and Clark Expedition.

Elderhostel participants enjoy a presentation on Northern Plains Indian culture administered by Blackfeet tribal member and local educator Don Fish. Here, participants learn a round dance in the Merici Lounge. Various items pertaining to explanation are on display in the room.

At the request of Bishop Brondel, the Ursuline Sisters founded the mission of St. Labre in eastern Montana in 1884. After almost 50 years of extreme hardship, their major superiors required them to leave. Today, the school is thriving in the Native American community. Pictured is part of the celebration of its 100th year. Many of the Ursulines were there to help celebrate with the Northern Cheyenne and Crow people.

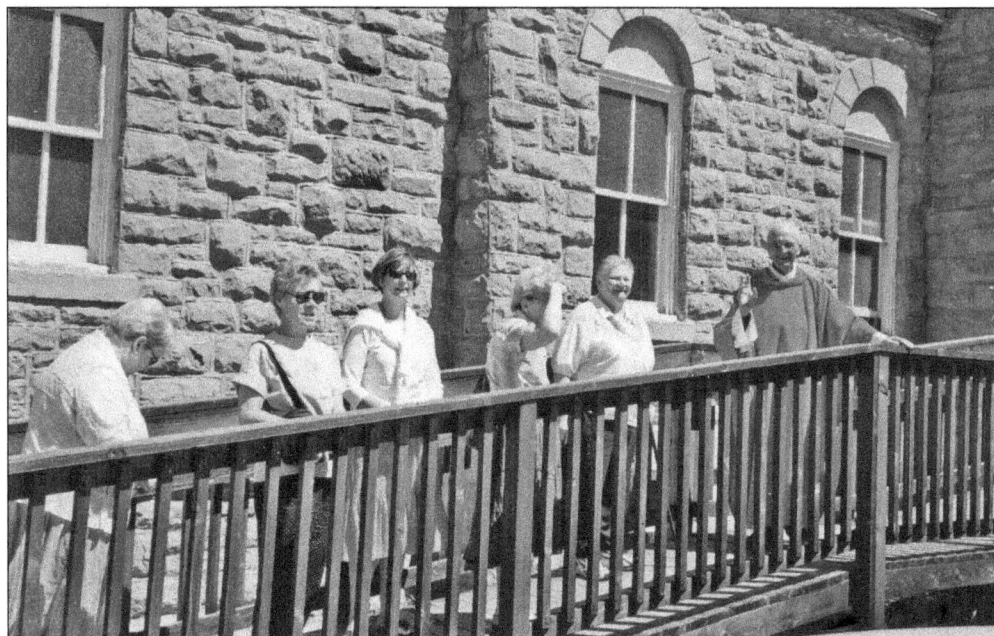

This group of sisters visits St. Paul's Mission, still an active parish and school in northern Montana. It is now staffed by Dominican sisters working with the Jesuit pastor.

A mystery theater and progressive dinner has been a popular program for Ursuline Centre since the late 1990s. Pictured here are longtime Ursuline employees Georges DiGeorgeo (who is dressed in character as the detective for the mystery theater) and Ursuline Centre assistant director Peggy Rowe.

An annual Mother's Day brunch and historic tour has become a tradition since 1996. Supporters of Ursuline Centre organize the function, which serves as a fundraiser for the center. The dessert room is a favorite stop at the mothers day brunch. Two attendees admire the selection.

AmeriCorps members pose for a photograph in the Heritage Museum. These young people come annually to stay at Ursuline Centre and utilize the building as a home base for their charitable work across the state. While there, they study with tax experts to master the codes enough to be able to travel to Indian reservations and offer help in filing income tax returns. Offering hospitality to such groups as AmeriCorps presents another opportunity for Ursuline Centre to reach out to the larger community. Through this program, Ursuline is able to contribute to a wide range of critical needs projects, including helping communities respond to disasters, tutoring disadvantaged youth, cleaning parks and streams, and building affordable housing.

A Native American-spirituality training group, Kateri, has met at Ursuline Centre for many years. Kateri Tekakwitha was a Mohawk woman who converted to Catholicism early in life and is in the process of being recognized as a saint by the Pope. She is the second American and the first Native American to be declared a saint. She has a large following of both Native Americans and non-Native Americans. This image of a Kateri prayer circle was captured in a meeting lounge on the first floor of Ursuline Centre in May 2012. The group came together from across the state for a Montana Missions Retreat. St. Peter's Mission is pictured in the large painting in the background.

In addition to many class reunions at Ursuline Academy, since the late 1950s, alumni from Central Catholic High School have celebrated part of a reunion weekend in Ursuline's chapel. Twice in recent years, Ursuline has had an all-school reunion. The reunions are substantial in size, as they include graduates from many classes. Pictured is a group from the class of 1970 on the steps of Ursuline Academy. Standing in front on the left is Fr. Anthony Gregori, who was a member of the faculty at Central Catholic High School for many years.

Ursuline Childcare and Preschool continues to offer children a value-based educational foundation in a Christian environment. Laypersons hold positions as certified teachers. The director has become a member of the board of trustees of Ursuline Centre. The program includes use of a computer, enabling educational programs to be part of the curriculum.

The Spanish Lingua program is an option for children whose parents desire to expose their child to a second language. Sessions are held a few days a week after the regular pre-kindergarten class.

122

Ursuline sisters believe that good education encompasses the whole person. This is true from the earliest years. Children in the preschool program are encouraged to share with each other, follow directions from the teacher, thank God for all their blessings, and learn letters and numbers. Time outside also provides opportunity for learning, fun, and physical activity.

Since Ursuline changed from an academy to a retreat and conference center, the number of nonprofit groups taking advantage of such a meeting place has grown annually. Below, the Donors' Plaza was created after the completion of a capital campaign to acknowledge those who had made generous contributions during the campaign. Its position in front of the main entrance calls attention to these donors, whose names are on a bench, planter, or on one of the bricks surrounding the centerpiece. In the center is an outline map of Montana with a star marking each place where Ursuline sisters served on an Indian mission. The cross in the center shows a list of the 145 Ursuline sisters who served in Great Falls.

In September 2011, supporters gather for the cutting of the Great Falls Chamber of Commerce ribbon. The occasion marked the laying of the cornerstone in 1911 and also the beginning of the Ursuline Centre Masonry Restoration project.

The century-old chapel at Ursuline Centre has changed little over time. The sisters made efforts to recognize it as a place of prayer, keeping it plain. The stained-glass windows induce calm, and the Stations of the Cross provide visual images to aid in reflection and prayer. The altar style has been made much less ornate in recent years, though the table is the same one used today.

Mass has been held in the chapel of Ursuline Centre for over one 100 years and continues to draw a small crowd. Pictured here are students in uniform on the left of the photograph. Parents and supporters sit or stand on the right side of the chapel's pews. Two Ursuline sisters can be seen among the kneelers on the far right in their dark habits, while servers and the priest are at the altar.

According to the reverse side, this photograph was taken in 1903 or 1904 and features Sister Annunciata in the midst of an open space. This Ursuline sister imparts a sense of quiet reflection, yet readiness to respond to new, yet undefined needs. Devotion to the love of Christ and striving to meet people's needs continue to be at the heart of Ursuline ministries. An account of 100 years of dedicated service and activity can have meaning only if one is led to the source—God.

BIBLIOGRAPHY

Mahoney, Irene, OSU *Lady Blackrobes: Missionaries in the Heart of Indian Country*. Golden: Fulcrum Publishing, 2006.

McBride, Genevieve, OSU *The Birdtail*. New York: Vantage Press, 1974.

Mount Angela Ursuline Academy. *The Link* Annals, 1912–1960. Great Falls, Montana.

Visit us at
arcadiapublishing.com

....

www.ingramcontent.com/pod-product-compliance
Lightning Source LLC
Chambersburg PA
CBHW050606110426
42813CB00008B/2471